More

Pizzazz

For Crayons and Wide Tipped Markers

Color With Angie & Friends

Join our friendly Color With Angie Grace Facebook group!

www.AngieGrace.com

Visit Angie's website for special web exclusives for colorists.

35585062R00060

Made in the USA
Lexington, KY
16 September 2014